# ANIMAINEIA

## by  Zach Lipman

osprey

A is for absolutely aerodynamic

black bears

B is for backyard barbecue

C  is for clumsy celebration

moose

dragonfly

D is for delicate daybreak

loon

E  is for ethereal enlightenment

F is for fabulously fragrant

skunk

pileated woodpecker

G is for gorgeous and glamorous

belted galloway cows

H  is for hardly homogenous

raccoon

I is for illuminated and incriminated

rock crabs

J is for jubilant jailbreakers

red foxes

K  is for keen kinship

bald eagle   humpack whale

L is for lofty levitation and large leviathan

Guernsey cow

M is for mooing moongazer

puffins

N  is for nautical noses

O is for orange October

tabby cat

seals

P  is for peeking pirate pups

red winged blackbirds

Q  is for quizzical queue

rainbow trout

R  is for relaxing rainbow

chickadee

S  is for serene sightseer

lobster

T is for teetotaling terrible tickler

gray squirrel

U is for unlawful and upside-down

hermit crab

V is for vacationing vagabond

sheep

W is for warm and woolly

gull

X is for coexisting

snowy owl

Y is for Yippee! Yahoo!

painted turtles

Z is for zany and zen

Made in the USA
Lexington, KY
17 April 2018